Dinosaurs

Kathleen Weidner Zoehfeld

NATIONAL
GEOGRAPHIC

Washington, D.C.

Published by Collins

An imprint of HarperCollins*Publishers*

The News Building

1 London Bridge Street

London

SE1 9GF

Browse the complete Collins catalogue at
www.collins.co.uk

In association with National Geographic Partners, LLC

NATIONAL GEOGRAPHIC and the Yellow Border Design are trademarks of the National Geographic Society, used under license.

Second edition 2018

First published 2011

ISBN 978-0-00-831719-5

10 9 8 7 6 5 4 3 2 1

A catalogue record for this book is available from the British Library

Printed by GPS, Slovenia

If you would like to comment on any aspect of this book, please contact us at the above address or online.

natgeokidsbooks.co.uk

cseducation@harpercollins.co.uk

Paper from responsible sources

Since 1888, the National Geographic Society has funded more than 12,000 research, exploration, and preservation projects around the world. The Society receives funds from National Geographic Partners, LLC, funded in part by your purchase. A portion of the proceeds from this book supports this vital work. To learn more, visit http://natgeo.com/info.

Photo Credits

All illustrations by Franco Tempesta unless otherwise noted below:

5, 32 (bottom, left): © Will Can Overbeek/ NationalGeographicStock.com; 6-9, 23, 32 (bottom, right): © Louie Psihoyos/ Corbis; 11 (top, left): © Brooks Walker/NationalGeographicStock.com; 11 (top, right): © Xu Xing; 18: © James Leynse/ Corbis; 20: © Francois Gohier/ Photo Researchers, Inc.; 26-27: © Karel Havlicek/ NationalGeographicStock.com; 28: © Joel Sartore/ NationalGeographicStock.com; 29: © National Geographic/ NationalGeographicStock. com; 31: © Paul Bricknell/Dorling Kindersley/ Getty Images; 32 (top, right): © Lynn Johnson/ NationalGeographicStock.com

Table of Contents

Big Scary Bones! 4

Digging Up Dinosaurs 6

Dinosaur Skin 10

Dinosaur Superstars 12

Smallest Dinosaurs 14

Biggest Dinosaurs 16

Walking on Tiptoes 18

What Did Dinosaurs Eat? 20

Dinosaur Mothers and Babies 24

Is THAT a Dinosaur? 26

Your Pet Dinosaur 30

Glossary 32

Big Scary Bones!

Have you ever seen dinosaur bones in a museum? Some of them are huge! If those bones came to life, it would be very scary.

But there's no need to worry. All the dinosaurs died off long, long ago.

The bones weren't always at the museum. Where did they come from?

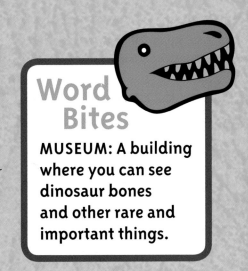

Word Bites

MUSEUM: A building where you can see dinosaur bones and other rare and important things.

Digging Up Dinosaurs

The dinosaur bones were buried safely in rock for a long time.

The bones are fossils. Paleontologists found them. They dug them out of the ground.

Word Bites

FOSSIL: Part of a living thing that has been saved in stone.

PALEONTOLOGIST: A scientist who finds and studies fossils.

Paleontologists brought the fossil bones to the museum and cleaned them. Then they put them all together.

The bones were on the inside of a dinosaur. But what did dinosaurs look like on the outside?

Dinosaur Skin

Sometimes dinosaur skin left prints in mud. The mud hardened and saved the prints.

These fossils tell us that some dinosaurs were scaly, like lizards.

Triceratops

Skin fossil

Feather fossil

Some dinosaurs had feathers, like birds.

Buitreraptor

Dinosaur Superstars

Tyrannosaurus rex was one of the biggest meat-eaters that ever walked the Earth.

Diplodocus was one of the longest dinosaurs ever found.

Pachycephalosaurus walked on two legs and had a thick, domed head.

Triceratops
had a huge head with three large horns and a wide neck frill.

Ankylosaurus
was an armoured dinosaur. It had a solid bone club at the end of its tail.

Stegosaurus
had rows of tall plates running down its back. Its tail had four deadly spikes.

Smallest Dinosaurs

We often think of dinosaurs as large and strong – but some dinosaurs were tiny.

Some were small enough to hold in your hands. Many small dinosaurs had feathers.

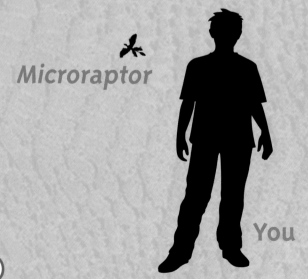

Microraptor

You

Microraptor

Biggest Dinosaurs

The biggest dinosaurs were the long-necked sauropods. You can't miss them!

Sauropods such as *Argentinosaurus* are the biggest land animals that ever lived.

Argentinosaurus

You

Argentinosaurus

Walking on Tiptoes

Knee

Big or small, scaly or feathery – all dinosaurs walked on their toes.

Ankle

Toes

Q How do you know when there's a dinosaur under your bed?

A Your nose hits the ceiling!

Also, all dinosaurs had curvy, S-shaped necks.

Neck

Edmontosaurus

What Did Dinosaurs Eat?

A dinosaur's teeth tell us what it ate. *Brachiosaurus* and *Diplodocus* were plant-eaters. Their teeth were good for snipping tough branches.

Fossil of *Diplodocus*

Brachiosaurus

Deinonychus

Other dinosaurs were meat-eaters. They ate other animals.

Deinonychus had teeth as sharp as steak knives. They were perfect for slicing meat.

Tooth of the meat-eater *Tyrannosaurus rex*

Dinosaur Mothers and Babies

All dinosaurs, even the scariest meat-eaters, laid eggs and had babies.

Dinosaurs like *Oviraptor* looked after their nests and kept their eggs warm. The babies hatched from the eggs. Then the parents looked after them until they were big enough to live on their own.

Oviraptor

Is THAT a Dinosaur?

Lots of people think anything big and extinct is a dinosaur. But that's not right.

Is this a dinosaur?

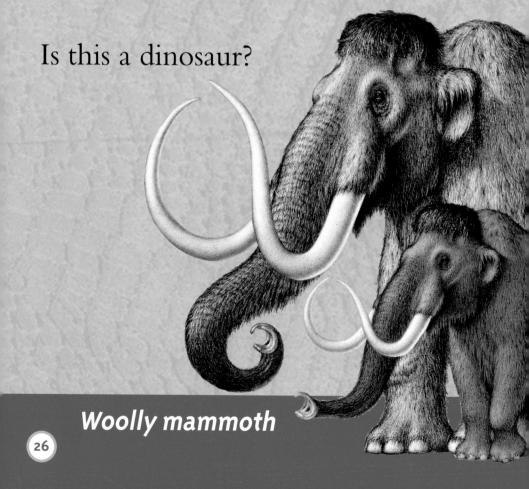

Woolly mammoth

No! The woolly mammoth was huge. But this animal did not lay eggs like a dinosaur. And it had fur. No dinosaurs had fur.

The woolly mammoth lived after the big dinosaurs went extinct.

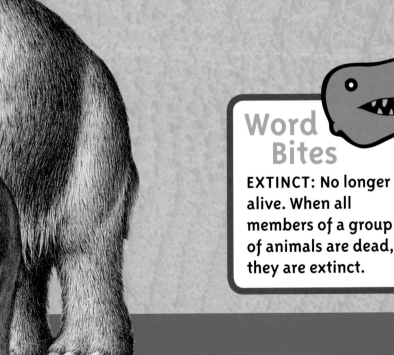

Word Bites

EXTINCT: No longer alive. When all members of a group of animals are dead, they are extinct.

Is this a dinosaur?

Chicken

It walks on its toes. It has a curvy neck. It has feathers like *Anchiornis*. And it lays eggs.

Yes! All birds are living dinosaurs.

Anchiornis

Your Pet Dinosaur

Many people would love to keep dinosaurs as pets.

You might think a *Tyrannosaurus rex* would be fun to play fetch with. But you wouldn't want to be near it at dinnertime. And besides, it's extinct!

If you want a living dinosaur of your own, the nearest thing is probably a bird.

A small bird like a budgie makes a better pet than a *Tyrannosaurus rex*!

Glossary

EXTINCT: No longer alive. When all members of a group of animals are dead, they are extinct.

FOSSIL: Part of a living thing that has been saved in stone.

MUSEUM: A building where you can see dinosaur bones and other rare and important things.

PALEONTOLOGIST: A scientist who finds and studies fossils.